Book D

Specific Skill Series

Locating the Answer

Richard A. Boning

Fifth Edition

SRA/McGraw-Hill

Columbus, Ohio

SRA/McGraw-Hill

*A Division of The **McGraw·Hill** Companies*

Send all inquiries to:
    SRA/McGraw-Hill
    8787 Orion Place
    Columbus, OH 43240-4027

ISBN 0-02-687954-9

    11   12   IPC   03

To the Teacher

PURPOSE:

As its title indicates, LOCATING THE ANSWER develops pupils' skill in finding *where* sought-for information can be found within a passage. Pupils must carefully read and understand each question, grasp phrase and sentence units, and discriminate between pertinent and irrelevant ideas.

FOR WHOM:

The skill of LOCATING THE ANSWER is developed through a series of books spanning ten levels (Picture, Preparatory, A, B, C, D, E, F, G, H). The Picture Level is for pupils who have not acquired a basic sight vocabulary. The Preparatory Level is for pupils who have a basic sight vocabulary but are not yet ready for the first-grade-level book. Books A through H are appropriate for pupils who can read on levels one through eight, respectively. **The use of the *Specific Skill Series Placement Test* is recommended to determine the appropriate level.**

THE NEW EDITION:

The fifth edition of the *Specific Skill Series* maintains the quality and focus that has distinguished this program for more than 25 years. A key element central to the program's success has been the unique nature of the reading selections. Nonfiction pieces about current topics have been designed to stimulate the interest of students, motivating them to use the comprehension strategies they have learned to further their reading. To keep this important aspect of the program intact, a percentage of the reading selections have been replaced in order to ensure the continued relevance of the subject material.

In addition, a significant percentage of the artwork in the program has been replaced to give the books a contemporary look. The cover photographs are designed to appeal to readers of all ages.

SESSIONS:

Short practice sessions are the most effective. It is desirable to have a practice session every day or every other day, using a few units each session.

To the Teacher

SCORING:

Pupils should record their answers on the reproducible worksheets. The worksheets make scoring easier and provide uniform records of the pupils' work. Using worksheets also avoids consuming the exercise books.

It is important for pupils to know how well they are doing. For this reason, units should be scored as soon as they have been completed. Then a discussion can be held in which pupils justify their choices. (The Integrated Language Activities, many of which are open-ended, do not lend themselves to an objective score; thus there are no answer keys for these pages.)

GENERAL INFORMATION ON *LOCATING THE ANSWER*:

At the earlier levels the answer to the question is worded much the same as the question itself. As the books increase in difficulty, there is less correspondence between the phrasing of the question and the phrasing of the answer.

SUGGESTED STEPS:

1. Pupils read the question *first* and then look for the answer.

2. Pupils use the range finder (sentence choices) in Books B–H. The letters or numbers in the range finder (below the question) indicate which sentences must be read to locate the answer to the question. In the Picture Level, the pupils decide which picture answers the question. For Preparatory and A levels, the number before the question tells the paragraph to read.

3. Pupils read the sentences with the question in mind. (On the Picture Level, pupils look at the pictures. On the Preparatory and A levels, pupils read the paragraph.)

4. When using Books B–H, pupils write (in the space on the worksheet) the letter or number of the sentence that answers the question. On the Picture Level, pupils write the letter of the correct picture choice. On the Preparatory and A levels, pupils write the letter of the correct word choice.

Additional information on using LOCATING THE ANSWER with pupils will be found in the **Specific Skill Series Teacher's Manual**.

RELATED MATERIALS:

Specific Skill Series Placement Tests, which enable the teacher to place pupils at their appropriate levels in each skill, are available for the Elementary (Pre-1–6) and Midway (4–8) grade levels.

About This Book

People read for different reasons. You may read a story just for fun. You may read a letter from a friend to find out what your friend has been doing. You may read a book to find the answer to a question.

Reading to find information is different from other reading. You are reading with a certain purpose. This means that you have to know what you are looking for. You need to read with your questions in mind. You can think of this as searching for something you have lost. You don't know where the lost object is, but you know what you are looking for.

Knowing what you are looking for can help you decide where to look. You wouldn't look for a missing shoe in the refrigerator. You might look for it under your bed or in the closet. You wouldn't look for the answer to a question about whales in a paragraph about dolphins. You would try to find the answer in a paragraph about whales.

Knowing how to locate information is an important reading skill. For each unit in this book, you will find ten questions about a piece of writing. The answers to the questions are in that piece of writing. Your job is to find where these answers are. You do not answer the questions. Instead, you tell **where** to find the answers.

Read this paragraph. Which sentence answers the question "Where do saltwater fish live?"

(**A**) There are two main groups of fish. (**B**) They are the saltwater fish and the freshwater fish. (**C**) Saltwater fish live in the oceans. (**D**) Freshwater fish live in streams, ponds, and lakes.

The answer is in sentence (**C**). Did you find it?

In each unit of this book, read the questions first. Look at the four letters below each question. Then look for the answer in the sentences with those four letters in the piece of writing. Read the sentences with the question in mind. Tell which sentence gives the answer.

(A) Did anyone ever tell you, "If you dig a hole deep enough, you'll reach China"? (B) China is on the opposite side of the earth from the United States. (C) No one can really dig all the way through the earth. (D) But if we could, we would reach China.

(E) China is the third largest country in the world. (F) Only Canada and Russia are bigger. (G) China covers over 3½ million square miles of land. (H) It is a little larger than the United States.

(I) However, China is much more crowded than the United States. (J) It has over a billion people—five times as many as the United States. (K) Millions more babies are born every year.

(L) China is one of the oldest countries in the world. (M) Its history goes back 3,500 years. (N) In those days the Chinese believed that the world was an island, with China in the center. (O) For this reason they have always called their country *Chung Kuo*, which means Middle Country.

(P) Over thousands of years the way of life of China's people changed very little, until modern times. (Q) Even today many Chinese still use animals or people to plow land or haul loads. (R) But more and more factories, railroads, and power plants are now being built. (S) More farms are getting tractors and electricity. (T) China is working hard to become as modern as the United States, Japan, or Europe.

(U) With all its people to feed, China is lucky to have much good farming land. (V) There, great amounts of rice, wheat, and other crops are grown. (W) Yet elsewhere in China very little can be grown. (X) The west contains mostly mountains and deserts. (Y) China's deserts are the driest in the world. (Z) The Himalaya Mountains on China's southern border are the highest in the world.

UNIT 1
A Land on the Other Side of the World

1. In relation to the United States, where is China located?
   Sentence **(A)**   **(B)**   **(C)**   **(D)**

2. Is Russia larger than China?
   Sentence **(E)**   **(F)**   **(G)**   **(H)**

3. How many babies are born yearly in China?
   Sentence **(I)**   **(J)**   **(K)**   **(L)**

4. Is China a very old country?
   Sentence **(J)**   **(K)**   **(L)**   **(M)**

5. Was China thought to be the central part of an island?
   Sentence **(M)**   **(N)**   **(O)**   **(P)**

6. How does one say *Middle Country* in Chinese?
   Sentence **(N)**   **(O)**   **(P)**   **(Q)**

7. Is there industry in China now?
   Sentence **(Q)**   **(R)**   **(S)**   **(T)**

8. Is China as modern as Japan?
   Sentence **(S)**   **(T)**   **(U)**   **(V)**

9. Does China have good farmland?
   Sentence **(U)**   **(V)**   **(W)**   **(X)**

10. Are there any deserts in China?
    Sentence **(W)**   **(X)**   **(Y)**   **(Z)**

UNIT 2
Living in China

(A) China's billion people have many different ways of living. (B) Most Chinese families live on farms. (C) The father, mother, and children often work together in the rice fields. (D) These fields, called paddies, are flooded with water so that the rice will grow. (E) The grandparents live with the family and help with cooking and other chores. (F) The Chinese believe it is very important for families to stay together.

(G) In China's cities life is very crowded. (H) Shanghai is one of the world's biggest cities. (I) It has over fourteen million people—far more than London or Chicago. (J) Like most big cities, Shanghai has traffic jams—but not from cars. (K) Many Chinese cannot afford cars. (L) Instead, they ride bicycles to work. (M) In Shanghai bicycles cause more traffic jams than cars.

(N) In the west of China, away from such big cities, life is far from crowded. (O) Much of the land is sandy or rocky, and few people live there. (P) People and goods still travel many places by camel or donkey. (Q) Some western Chinese live in round tents called yurts.

(R) The Chinese "alphabet" has over forty thousand "letters"! (S) That is because each "letter" stands for a whole word. (T) Chinese kids do learn to read and write, inspite of all those letters!

(U) One of the favorite sports in China is table tennis. (V) Since it needs little space and little equipment, nearly everyone can play—and play well. (W) Chinese table tennis players are often world champions. (X) The Chinese also enjoy cooking—and eating. (Y) Their menus may include cold jellyfish, boiled duck, pigeon eggs, and shark fins. (Z) Somehow, they make it all taste delicious.

UNIT 2
Living in China

1. Do most Chinese families live in cities?
   Sentence   (A)   (B)   (C)   (D)

2. Does the mother often have an office job?
   Sentence   (B)   (C)   (D)   (E)

3. Do the people in a Chinese family usually stay close together?
   Sentence   (D)   (E)   (F)   (G)

4. Where in China are there crowded conditions?
   Sentence   (G)   (H)   (I)   (J)

5. How do most Chinese people get to work?
   Sentence   (K)   (L)   (M)   (N)

6. Besides the donkey, what animal is used for travel?
   Sentence   (N)   (O)   (P)   (Q)

7. Do Chinese children learn more than twenty-six letters?
   Sentence   (Q)   (R)   (S)   (T)

8. What sport is a favorite in China?
   Sentence   (S)   (T)   (U)   (V)

9. Are the Chinese among the best in the world at table tennis?
   Sentence   (U)   (V)   (W)   (X)

10. Is eating boring to the Chinese?
    Sentence   (W)   (X)   (Y)   (Z)

(A) What do you think is the greatest structure ever built? (B) It is the Great Wall of China. (C) This wall stretches across most of northern China. (D) It is over two thousand miles long. (E) It rises higher than a two-story house. (F) Yet it was built entirely by hand!

(G) The Great Wall also took longer to build than any other structure. (H) It was started by a Chinese ruler, Ch'in, over 2,200 years ago. (I) The last parts were built about 1,700 years later!

(J) Of course, there were no trucks or machines in those days. (K) Hundreds of thousands of Chinese were forced to haul earth and stones to build the Wall. (L) Thousands died on the job. (M) The Wall became their gravestone.

(N) The Wall winds over mountains and valleys, from the ocean to the desert. (O) It is so thick that a road runs along the top. (P) About every five hundred feet along the Wall there is a tower. (Q) In some places, where stone was scarce, the Wall was built of packed earth. (R) Much of this part is in ruins today. (S) Elsewhere, stone was carefully cut into blocks for the face of the Wall. (T) It is said that if the blocks didn't fit closely enough, the stonecutter's head was chopped off.

(U) We are not sure just why the Wall was built. (V) One reason probably was to keep enemies out of China. (W) Yet it was not very difficult for enemy soldiers to climb over the Wall, and they often did. (X) The ruler Ch'in may have started the Wall to give work to thousands of Chinese who needed jobs. (Y) Perhaps Ch'in just wanted it to mark the border of China. (Z) Some experts believe that Ch'in wanted to build the Wall all around China—over five thousand miles!

1. How long is the Great Wall of China?
   Sentence   (A)   (B)   (C)   (D)

2. Was the Great Wall built quickly?
   Sentence   (E)   (F)   (G)   (H)

3. Did Ch'in live to see the Wall completed?
   Sentence   (H)   (I)   (J)   (K)

4. Did the workers haul the earth and stone willingly?
   Sentence   (I)   (J)   (K)   (L)

5. What did the Wall become to many workers?
   Sentence   (K)   (L)   (M)   (N)

6. Is there a road near the Great Wall?
   Sentence   (M)   (N)   (O)   (P)

7. Besides stone, was any other material used?
   Sentence   (O)   (P)   (Q)   (R)

8. What was used to face the Wall?
   Sentence   (Q)   (R)   (S)   (T)

9. Was care used in fitting the blocks?
   Sentence   (S)   (T)   (U)   (V)

10. Did the Wall prevent enemies from entering China?
    Sentence   (W)   (X)   (Y)   (Z)

(A) Do you know what three countries make up Scandinavia? (B) They are Norway, Sweden, and Denmark. (C) These countries are located in northern Europe. (D) They are known for their natural beauty and for their cold weather.

(E) Norway is sometimes called "Land of the Midnight Sun." (F) How did Norway get this nickname? (G) One-third of the country lies above the Arctic Circle. (H) Since Norway is so far north, for ten weeks during the summer the sun shines all the time. (I) It even shines at midnight!

(J) Sweden is beautiful in its own way. (K) This country is located between Norway and Denmark. (L) Its northern mountains form Sweden's border with Norway. (M) The mountains have high, rocky, snow-covered peaks. (N) Sweden's coast is dotted with villages and has both rocky and sandy beaches. (O) Thousands of clear, blue lakes cover much of the middle part of the country.

(P) Denmark is almost completely surrounded by water. (Q) The country covers one peninsula and 482 islands. (R) There are also many small beautiful lakes and rivers in Denmark. (S) It is not surprising that fish is one of the favorite foods of the people of Denmark, who are called Danes.

(T) Sports are very important in all of Scandinavia. (U) In Norway and Sweden skiing is not just a fun sport. (V) In snow-covered places it is actually the best way to get around! (W) Many great hockey and soccer stars have also come from the Scandinavian countries.

(X) The water and mountains together create much natural beauty. (Y) People can climb mountains, ski, swim, or just walk around the countryside. (Z) Perhaps that is why so many visitors brave the cold to visit this land of beauty!

1. What countries are in Scandinavia?
    Sentence **(A)**   **(B)**   **(C)**   **(D)**

2. Is Norway above the Arctic Circle?
    Sentence **(E)**   **(F)**   **(G)**   **(H)**

3. Where does the sun shine all the time?
    Sentence **(G)**   **(H)**   **(I)**   **(J)**

4. Is Sweden a lovely country, too?
    Sentence **(I)**   **(J)**   **(K)**   **(L)**

5. Where is Sweden located?
    Sentence **(K)**   **(L)**   **(M)**   **(N)**

6. Is Denmark located near water?
    Sentence **(M)**   **(N)**   **(O)**   **(P)**

7. What is one of Denmark's most popular foods?
    Sentence **(P)**   **(Q)**   **(R)**   **(S)**

8. Do people ski in Norway and Sweden?
    Sentence **(T)**   **(U)**   **(V)**   **(W)**

9. What gives Scandinavia its beauty?
    Sentence **(V)**   **(W)**   **(X)**   **(Y)**

10. Is Scandinavia a popular place to visit?
    Sentence **(W)**   **(X)**   **(Y)**   **(Z)**

UNIT 5
Holland, a Watery Land

(A) Holland lies at the edge of the North Sea, on the northwestern coast of Europe. (B) Sometimes this flat, watery land is called the Netherlands. (C) The people of Holland are known as Dutch, Netherlanders, or Hollanders.

(D) Holland is small but is one of the most crowded countries in the world. (E) It is about thirteen times as crowded as the United States. (F) Yet the total number of people is much smaller. (G) By using land that was once covered by water, the Dutch now have a little more space in which to live.

(H) Holland has a mild, damp climate. (I) There is rain or fog for more than half the year. (J) But the rain is not heavy, nor does it last long. (K) Holland receives about twenty-five inches of rainfall each year. (L) For the most part, the winters are not too cold and the summers are pleasantly cool. (M) This climate makes Holland the perfect place for raising dairy cattle. (N) The mild temperature and the frequent rains help to provide fine grass for the cattle. (O) The farmers get plenty of rich milk from the cows. (P) Much of the milk is made into cheese and butter, some of which is shipped to other countries.

(Q) The Dutch have many waterways. (R) The waterways run through Holland and link it to Belgium and Germany. (S) Three of the most important rivers are the Rhine, Maas, and Scheldt. (T) It is clear why Holland has become an important shipping center. (U) The port of Rotterdam is one of the busiest in Europe.

(V) Many raw materials have to be brought into Holland. (W) Its factories make them into finished products. (X) Holland's shipyards are excellent. (Y) Beautiful cloth comes from its textile mills. (Z) Its many factories prepare food for storage or shipment.

1. Along which body of water is Holland located?
   Sentence   **(A)**   **(B)**   **(C)**   **(D)**

2. What is another name for Holland?
   Sentence   **(B)**   **(C)**   **(D)**   **(E)**

3. Does Holland have more people than America?
   Sentence   **(C)**   **(D)**   **(E)**   **(F)**

4. How have the Dutch added living space?
   Sentence   **(F)**   **(G)**   **(H)**   **(I)**

5. Does Holland get any fog?
   Sentence   **(I)**   **(J)**   **(K)**   **(L)**

6. How many inches of rain fall in Holland each year?
   Sentence   **(K)**   **(L)**   **(M)**   **(N)**

7. What is the value of the rain?
   Sentence   **(N)**   **(O)**   **(P)**   **(Q)**

8. What are the names of some Dutch rivers?
   Sentence   **(Q)**   **(R)**   **(S)**   **(T)**

9. Is Rotterdam a port?
   Sentence   **(T)**   **(U)**   **(V)**   **(W)**

10. What comes from Holland's textile mills?
    Sentence   **(W)**   **(X)**   **(Y)**   **(Z)**

UNIT 6
Living in Holland

(A) Holland is the land of the bicycle. (B) Bicycles are stopping, starting, and whizzing along everywhere. (C) At rush hours the cities swarm with them. (D) There are a number of reasons why the bicycle is so popular. (E) The flatness of the land makes pedaling easy. (F) The fact that the country is so small and crowded makes the bicycle handy and ideal for traveling.

(G) With water everywhere around them, it is no wonder that the Dutch like water sports. (H) They can take their choice of lakes, ponds, canals, rivers, or even the North Sea. (I) Swimming and boating are popular. (J) In the winter the Netherlanders turn to ice-skating, the frozen-water sport. (K) They enjoy this most of all. (L) When the first big freeze comes, the Dutch take a holiday on ice.

(M) The Dutch people dress much like Americans. (N) In some parts of the country the villagers wear *klompen*, or wooden shoes. (O) Wooden shoes keep the feet drier than leather. (P) The old Dutch folk costumes are not worn much today, except in a few villages.

(Q) Like most people, the Hollanders are fond of food. (R) They especially like seafood, such as oysters, herring, and eel. (S) Cheeses are also popular, mainly Edam and Gouda. (T) The Dutch, especially the children, enjoy cakes and cookies, which they call *koeken* and *koejes*. (U) Thick, steaming pea soup is another favorite dish.

(V) Since wood is quite scarce, most homes in Holland are made of brick. (W) They are often painted bright colors. (X) The houses have big windows to let in as much sunlight as possible. (Y) Neat, well-cared-for gardens surround most of the homes. (Z) Pretty flowers not only add a touch of beauty to the homes, but also brighten up the whole landscape.

UNIT 6
Living in Holland

1. At what times are cities crowded with bicycles?
   Sentence   (A)   (B)   (C)   (D)

2. Why is pedaling a bicycle so easy in Holland?
   Sentence   (B)   (C)   (D)   (E)

3. What are two reasons why a bicycle is so handy?
   Sentence   (E)   (F)   (G)   (H)

4. Do the Dutch enjoy swimming?
   Sentence   (G)   (H)   (I)   (J)

5. In what season do the Dutch go ice-skating?
   Sentence   (J)   (K)   (L)   (M)

6. What are *klompen*?
   Sentence   (K)   (L)   (M)   (N)

7. What seafoods do the Dutch like?
   Sentence   (P)   (Q)   (R)   (S)

8. What are *koejes*?
   Sentence   (S)   (T)   (U)   (V)

9. Why aren't many homes made of wood?
   Sentence   (U)   (V)   (W)   (X)

10. Why do the houses have large windows?
    Sentence   (W)   (X)   (Y)   (Z)

Like most people, the Hollanders are fond of food. They especially like seafood, such as oysters, herring, and eel. Cheeses are also popular, mainly Edam and Gouda. The Dutch, especially the children, enjoy cakes and cookies, which they call *koeken* and *koejes*. Thick, steaming pea soup is another favorite dish.

A. Exercising Your Skill

The paragraph above tells about foods that the people of Holland (the Dutch) like to eat. Look for books in your school library to find out more information about Holland. For example, you may find out about other kinds of food. You may also find information about the country's other products, cities, or climate. On your paper, list up to five other kinds of things the book tells you about Holland.

B. Expanding Your Skill

The library arranges books in different sections or shelves by topic, or subject. Look at the library map below. It shows how books on these subjects might be arranged.

	Door	
Sea Animals Section	Desk	**Stars and Planets Section**
Land Animals Section		**Weather Section**
Birds Section		**Farm Crops Section**

Now write the numbers 1 through 6 on your paper. Then write the name of the section where you would look to find a book that would answer each question.

1. Is the planet Pluto smaller than Jupiter?
2. Does Holland have many hurricanes?
3. How are eagles and ostriches different?
4. What food crops are grown in China?
5. What kinds of animals live in the Himalaya Mountains?
6. How do dolphins "talk" to each other?

C. Exploring Language

Read the following paragraphs about two places in China—the Himalayas, a mountain range, and the Gobi Desert. On your paper, write six questions that can be answered after reading each of these paragraphs. Write three questions for each paragraph.

The Himalayas lie in the southwestern part of China. Mt. Everest, the highest mountain in the world, is part of the Himalayas. Icy glaciers, rivers, lakes, and forests are all part of the Himalayas. Many animals live here. Elephants, buffalos, and black bears live in the forests. Snow leopards and Tibetan yaks live in the higher areas, where there are few or no trees.

The Gobi Desert lies partly along the northern border of China. This desert is mostly flat land, but it has a few flat-topped hills. One part of the Gobi is waterless, but most of the desert has some water. A few shallow lakes provide some of this water. In other areas, water is taken from wells. Grass and scrub bushes grow on much of the desert. Wandering herders make the Gobi their home and feed their animals on the plant life.

D. Expressing Yourself

Choose one of these activities.

1. Get together with four or five classmates. Take turns being "questioner." The first questioner should ask a question from a page in a social studies book that everyone has. See who can find the answer on the page first. Continue until each group member has been the questioner.

2. Draw a map of part of your school. Label the different areas. Then name things like books, food, or sports equipment. As you name something, ask a classmate to tell in which area that thing would be found and why.

UNIT 7
At War with the Sea

(A) The Dutch have been at war with the sea from earliest times. (B) For centuries the sea has flooded parts of their land. (C) This is not only because of Holland's location by the sea. (D) Many countries have grown up next to the ocean. (E) But Holland is the only country with half its land below sea level. (F) This has put Holland at the mercy of the sea.

(G) The Dutch have fought back. (H) At first they built low, earthen walls that did not last long. (I) In time, they learned to build high, strong walls of stone and cement. (J) These walls are called dikes. (K) Some are fifty feet tall. (L) The Dutch have worked hard to stop the ocean from robbing them of more land. (M) They also have worked to get back the land the sea has already taken.

(N) Long ago the ocean smashed into Holland and formed a big saltwater lake called the Zuider Zee. (O) The Dutch decided to cut off the lake from the North Sea. (P) They built a dike along the coastal edge of the lake. (Q) Then they pumped part of the lake dry. (R) The drained fields are called *polders*. (S) They are used for farms and houses. (T) Now half the people of Holland live on land that was once underwater.

(U) The Dutch have also built dikes to hold back the rivers. (V) They have built dams across the rivers to close them off from the sea. (W) Rivers can also flood the land.

(X) Holland's war with the sea is a war of walls, not bullets. (Y) It is a war which the Dutch must win. (Z) It is a war that will go on just as long as there is an ocean and a Holland.

1. Has the sea flooded Holland for centuries?
    Sentence   **(A)**   **(B)**   **(C)**   **(D)**

2. How much of Holland is below sea level?
    Sentence   **(C)**   **(D)**   **(E)**   **(F)**

3. At first, what kind of walls did the Dutch build?
    Sentence   **(E)**   **(F)**   **(G)**   **(H)**

4. What are the walls called?
    Sentence   **(I)**   **(J)**   **(K)**   **(L)**

5. Is the Zuider Zee a river?
    Sentence   **(L)**   **(M)**   **(N)**   **(O)**

6. What did the Dutch build on the lake's edge?
    Sentence   **(N)**   **(O)**   **(P)**   **(Q)**

7. What are *polders*?
    Sentence   **(P)**   **(Q)**   **(R)**   **(S)**

8. How are *polders* used by the Dutch?
    Sentence   **(R)**   **(S)**   **(T)**   **(U)**

9. Can rivers flood the land?
    Sentence   **(T)**   **(U)**   **(V)**   **(W)**

10. How long will Holland's war go on?
    Sentence   **(W)**   **(X)**   **(Y)**   **(Z)**

(A) For centuries the rest of the world knew little about India. (B) Because of its position, India had been cut off from contact with most other nations. (C) The country is a triangle of land in central Asia. (D) Along the top of the triangle, on the border with China, are the Himalayas. (E) These are the highest mountains in the world. (F) The bottom of the triangle points out into the Indian Ocean.

(G) The Himalayas have barred outsiders from coming into India. (H) They have also kept rainstorms from getting out. (I) As a result, the northern part of India receives a great deal of rain. (J) During the monsoon, or rainy season, as much as a hundred inches of rain may fall in three months. (K) The northern part of India is the largest area of farmland in the world.

(L) More than six out of every ten people in India are farmers. (M) They grow large amounts of cotton and jute. (N) These crops are woven into cloths or textiles. (O) The large cities, such as Delhi, Calcutta, and Bombay, contain textile mills. (P) India is also a world leader in growing peanuts, pepper, and tea.

(Q) Despite large crops, India finds it difficult to feed its people. (R) Next to China, India has the largest population in the world. (S) It is about one third the size of the United States, but it contains four times as many people. (T) It is good news that new farming methods are being introduced. (U) In many villages, small manufacturing plants are being started.

(V) However, ancient ways die slowly. (W) India is still a land where many people live in huts, far out in the countryside. (X) In places like these, people often do things the same way they did a hundred years ago. (Y) They have not caught up with the modern world. (Z) In many ways, India is still an unknown land.

1. In the past, has India had much contact with other countries?
    Sentence   (**A**)   (**B**)   (**C**)   (**D**)

2. Are the Himalayas the highest mountains in the world?
    Sentence   (**D**)   (**E**)   (**F**)   (**G**)

3. Does the north have much rain?
    Sentence   (**G**)   (**H**)   (**I**)   (**J**)

4. What is the rainy season called?
    Sentence   (**I**)   (**J**)   (**K**)   (**L**)

5. Where is the largest area of farmland in the world?
    Sentence   (**K**)   (**L**)   (**M**)   (**N**)

6. Are many people farmers?
    Sentence   (**L**)   (**M**)   (**N**)   (**O**)

7. What is done with jute?
    Sentence   (**M**)   (**N**)   (**O**)   (**P**)

8. Does India grow tea?
    Sentence   (**O**)   (**P**)   (**Q**)   (**R**)

9. Does any nation have a larger population than India?
    Sentence   (**P**)   (**Q**)   (**R**)   (**S**)

10. Is India changing rapidly?
    Sentence   (**S**)   (**T**)   (**U**)   (**V**)

UNIT 9
Living in India

(A) Life has changed little in much of India. (B) A person who had lived there a thousand years ago and returned today might feel right at home. (C) Three out of four people still live in small villages. (D) They usually live in mud or straw huts without electricity or running water. (E) They still work the small farms outside the villages. (F) In almost every way they follow the customs of their parents and grandparents.

(G) Many people in India do not put their money in banks. (H) Instead, they buy jewelry. (I) Women fasten gems to their noses. (J) Both men and women wear jeweled bracelets around their wrists and ankles. (K) The more jewelry a family has, the more wealthy it is considered to be.

(L) India has long been famous for its beautiful fabrics. (M) Many people wear only one piece of outer clothing. (N) This is a cloth wrapped around the body. (O) It is often made of cotton or silk. (P) A woman's cloth, called a *sari*, is long and brightly colored.

(Q) There are more festivals in India than anywhere else in the world. (R) Holi, a popular holiday, welcomes spring. (S) Young and old celebrate with an unusual custom. (T) They squirt colored water on each other. (U) By the end of the day, everyone is blazing with color.

(V) Much of India is a land of the past, but it is slowly changing. (W) In many villages people now ride bicycles. (X) Radios are becoming popular. (Y) News of the outside world can now reach the entire nation. (Z) With growing knowledge, the people of India look forward to a better tomorrow.

UNIT 9
Living in India

1. How many people live in small villages?
   Sentence   **(A)**   **(B)**   **(C)**   (D)

2. Where are the farms located?
   Sentence   **(D)**   **(E)**   **(F)**   (G)

3. Where do men and women wear bracelets?
   Sentence   **(G)**   **(H)**   **(I)**   (J)

4. Is India well known for cloth?
   Sentence   **(K)**   **(L)**   **(M)**   (N)

5. What is a woman's cloth called?
   Sentence   **(M)**   **(N)**   **(O)**   (P)

6. Are there many festivals in India?
   Sentence   **(Q)**   **(R)**   **(S)**   (T)

7. Do young and old celebrate spring?
   Sentence   **(R)**   **(S)**   **(T)**   (U)

8. Is much of India a land of the present?
   Sentence   **(U)**   **(V)**   **(W)**   (X)

9. How do people learn about the outside world?
   Sentence   **(V)**   **(W)**   **(X)**   (Y)

10. Is knowledge increasing?
    Sentence   **(W)**   **(X)**   **(Y)**   (Z)

(**A**) In the city of Agra, India, there is a building that amazes builders the world over. (**B**) It is the Taj Mahal. (**C**) It is made entirely of marble. (**D**) Yet it looks so light and graceful that it appears to float in air. (**E**) Modern builders admit, "Today we do not have workers that are skilled enough to make such a building. (**F**) Truly, it is a miracle in marble."

(**G**) The Taj Mahal was built more than three hundred years ago. (**H**) Yet it looks so new that it could have been built yesterday. (**I**) The building rises two hundred feet from a large marble platform. (**J**) It is set in a square over three hundred feet long and three hundred feet wide. (**K**) The roof is round. (**L**) In the moonlight it glows like a giant pearl. (**M**) A long pool before the building acts as a mirror.

(**N**) Shah Jahan built the Taj as a tomb for his wife, Mumtaz Mahal. (**O**) Expert workers fitted pieces of marble together in beautiful patterns and designs. (**P**) Many of the pieces were inlaid with jewels. (**Q**) It is impossible to tell where the stones in these designs are joined.

(**R**) The Taj Mahal is just as beautiful on the inside as it is on the outside. (**S**) The walls are covered with pure gold. (**T**) Doors are of solid silver. (**U**) A covering of ten thousand pearls hangs over the tomb of the empress. (**V**) Many treasures have been stolen, but a number remain. (**W**) It is estimated that it took twenty thousand people more than twenty years to complete this amazing structure.

(**X**) "Even if we had the skill," say modern builders, "we could not build a Taj Mahal today. (**Y**) No one could afford it. (**Z**) It would cost more than the combined cost of all the leading skyscrapers in America."

Miracle in Marble

1. Is the Taj Mahal made completely of marble?
   Sentence   (A)   (B)   (C)   (D)

2. How do modern builders describe the Taj Mahal?
   Sentence   (E)   (F)   (G)   (H)

3. What shape does the roof have?
   Sentence   (H)   (I)   (J)   (K)

4. What does the roof do in the moonlight?
   Sentence   (L)   (M)   (N)   (O)

5. Why was the Taj Mahal built?
   Sentence   (N)   (O)   (P)   (Q)

6. What did the workers fit together?
   Sentence   (O)   (P)   (Q)   (R)

7. What do some of the pieces contain?
   Sentence   (P)   (Q)   (R)   (S)

8. Is the Taj Mahal lovely inside?
   Sentence   (Q)   (R)   (S)   (T)

9. Does the tomb have a special covering?
   Sentence   (S)   (T)   (U)   (V)

10. How long did it take to build the Taj Mahal?
    Sentence   (U)   (V)   (W)   (X)

UNIT 11
Antarctica: Land of Mystery

(**A**) Was there a land of mystery at the bottom of the world? (**B**) For centuries people had heard tales of such a land. (**C**) Yet it was not until 150 years ago that anyone was sure it existed. (**D**) A young Yankee skipper braved floating cakes of ice the size of the state of Delaware to find it. (**E**) That skipper was the first person in history to gaze upon the frozen land of Antarctica.

(**F**) Antarctica is a continent twice as large as the United States. (**G**) At one time it was a land of swamps and jungles. (**H**) Then, millions of years ago, the climate began to grow colder. (**I**) Snowfalls caused the plant life to freeze and finally disappear. (**J**) Now the continent is covered by ice as much as two miles thick. (**K**) Only a few spots are not covered by ice or snow.

(**L**) Temperatures in Antarctica are the lowest in the world. (**M**) The temperature often drops to eighty-five degrees below zero Fahrenheit! (**N**) It is so cold that there is very little animal life. (**O**) There are a few mosses and some birds, including penguins. (**P**) These are large birds that cannot fly. (**Q**) They walk upright and look like fat little people.

(**R**) Antarctica belongs to no one. (**S**) Many nations have claimed the land, but no one occupies it. (**T**) In 1959 twelve nations signed the Antarctic Treaty. (**U**) By this treaty these nations agreed that the area was to be used only for scientific purposes.

(**V**) The United States and other nations have set up weather stations there. (**W**) Scientists study the snow and ice. (**X**) They are attempting to find out what changed the climate so long ago. (**Y**) "When we do," they explain, "Antarctica will no longer be a land of mystery. (**Z**) We may even learn how to control the weather in the rest of the world."

1. Where did people think there was a land of mystery?
   Sentence   **(A)**   **(B)**   **(C)**   **(D)**

2. Had people heard tales of such a land?
   Sentence   **(B)**   **(C)**   **(D)**   **(E)**

3. Was there ever any swampland in Antarctica?
   Sentence   **(E)**   **(F)**   **(G)**   **(H)**

4. What did the snowfalls do to the plant life?
   Sentence   **(I)**   **(J)**   **(K)**   **(L)**

5. Does the temperature drop far below zero?
   Sentence   **(K)**   **(L)**   **(M)**   **(N)**

6. Are there many animals in this region?
   Sentence   **(M)**   **(N)**   **(O)**   **(P)**

7. Do penguins fly?
   Sentence   **(P)**   **(Q)**   **(R)**   **(S)**

8. When was the Antarctic Treaty signed?
   Sentence   **(Q)**   **(R)**   **(S)**   **(T)**

9. For what purpose is the land to be used?
   Sentence   **(T)**   **(U)**   **(V)**   **(W)**

10. Do scientists call Antarctica "the land of mystery"?
    Sentence   **(W)**   **(X)**   **(Y)**   **(Z)**

(A) Scientists at the South Pole station live in a city unlike any other in the world. (B) This city is a weather station, right on the pole itself. (C) Here the winds blow at rates up to two hundred miles per hour. (D) Buildings are quickly covered with snow. (E) In seconds the snow blinds people and causes them to get lost and die. (F) To escape the wind, the scientists at the South Pole station have carved out a city beneath the surface of the ice.

(G) Only the hardiest scientists are able to live here. (H) A private bedroom is provided for each person. (I) So the scientists will keep fit and happy, they are given the finest food. (J) They can see movies in a theater under the ice. (K) They can send and receive mail at the post office. (L) All these rooms and offices are connected by tunnels.

(M) Each day researchers must journey to the surface. (N) There they conduct their studies. (O) This is a dangerous trip. (P) For protection, they travel to the surface in pairs. (Q) On the surface, a person can freeze to death without even knowing it. (R) They watch each other closely for telltale patches of snow-white skin. (S) This is the first mark of frostbite. (T) A sudden snowstorm may come up. (U) It can be so blinding that people may lose their way just a few feet from the door to the underground city. (V) Scientists use guide ropes to find their way back to the door.

(W) During the winter, this is a land of total darkness. (X) When summer comes, the scientists are able to go home. (Y) The storms die down, and it is safe for airplanes to land. (Z) Few people can endure more than one winter in the city below the ice.

1. Where is the South Pole station?
   Sentence   (A)   (B)   (C)   (D)

2. How strong is the wind?
   Sentence   (B)   (C)   (D)   (E)

3. At the Pole, what does the snow do to people?
   Sentence   (E)   (F)   (G)   (H)

4. Why are the scientists given especially good food?
   Sentence   (G)   (H)   (I)   (J)

5. Is there a post office at the station?
   Sentence   (I)   (J)   (K)   (L)

6. Is travel to the surface dangerous?
   Sentence   (M)   (N)   (O)   (P)

7. Would a person who is freezing to death feel it?
   Sentence   (P)   (Q)   (R)   (S)

8. Do snowstorms come up suddenly?
   Sentence   (S)   (T)   (U)   (V)

9. Would the blinding snow cause anyone to get lost?
   Sentence   (U)   (V)   (W)   (X)

10. Can many people stay in the city for more than one winter?
    Sentence   (W)   (X)   (Y)   (Z)

A. Exercising Your Skill

In Units 8, 9, and 10, you read about life in India. These passages could have been skimmed or scanned for information. When you **scan**, you move your eyes quickly over the writing to find certain facts you are looking for. When you **skim**, you read quickly to find the main idea of the writing.

Number your paper from 1 to 5. Read the following questions. Write *scan* or *skim* next to the number to tell how you would read to locate the answer to that question.

1. How many people live in Calcutta?
2. Why couldn't the Taj Mahal be built today?
3. What percentage of Indian people are farmers?
4. What is a sari?
5. Why do Indian people value jewelry?

B. Expanding Your Skill

Read the following paragraph about the Taj Mahal. On your paper, create a fact wheel like the one below. Locate facts in the paragraph to finish the phrases.

> The Taj Mahal was built more than three hundred years ago. It was built by Shah Jahan in memory of his beloved wife, Mumtaz Mahal. The all-marble structure, which took more than twenty years to build, rises two hundred feet from a large platform. A long pool in front of the monument reflects its pearl-like beauty.

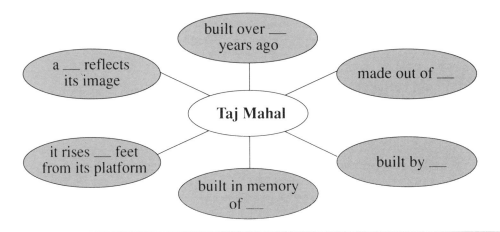

C. Exploring Language

Read the following paragraph. On your paper answer the questions with full sentences. The information is in the paragraph. You can use your own words.

Mother Teresa began working as a high school teacher in Calcutta. She was aware, however, of the masses of poor and sick people in that city. She knew that many adults, and especially children, lived and died on the streets of Calcutta. Mother Teresa left her teaching job and started the Missionary Sisters of Charity to help Calcutta's poor and sick. She brought children in from the streets and educated them. She also started a place where dying poor people could come for shelter and care. This place was called "Place of the Pure Heart."

1. What work did Mother Teresa do first in Calcutta?
2. What happened to many people on the streets of Calcutta?
3. Who did Mother Teresa help with her missionary work?
4. Who did Mother Teresa help with the "Place of the Pure Heart"?

D. Expressing Yourself

Choose one of these activities.

1. Look in the travel section of a Sunday newspaper. Cut out one or two paragraphs about a place that interests you. Write five questions that can be answered by scanning the material. Ask a classmate to scan and find the answers. See how long it takes your classmate.

2. Choose a partner. Then make up a word maze game. Hide words in rows of letters. Give clues to each word. See how long it takes your partner to find each word. Here is one example.

(clues) I am huge. I "carry" a trunk. I am an _____ .
(maze) a o t h p e r t e l e p h a n t o p i k

(**A**) Why are so many scientists interested in life in Antarctica? (**B**) Most plant and animal life died out after ice covered the continent millions of years ago. (**C**) Yet a few living things are strong enough to live in this cold. (**D**) They are unusual, so scientists want to know more about them.

(**E**) Plants and land animals are very rare in Antarctica. (**F**) Scientists have found only three kinds of flowering plants. (**G**) Trees and bushes cannot grow in the thick layer of ice that covers the land. (**H**) Explorers have found fossils of other kinds of plants and wood. (**I**) They can tell that before the ice came, other plants grew there. (**J**) The largest land animal (that is an animal that lives *only* on land and not also in the water) is an insect similar to the housefly. (**K**) This insect is only one-tenth of an inch long!

(**L**) In Antarctica, most animals live in the ocean all or some of the time. (**M**) There are many kinds of whales. (**N**) The killer whale and the blue whale are probably the most well known. (**O**) The blue whale is the largest creature that has ever lived. (**P**) It can grow as long as 100 feet. (**Q**) Many people are afraid of the blue whale, but it doesn't even have any teeth!

(**R**) Seals are one of the most playful ocean animals (**S**) Of the six kinds of seals that live in Antarctica, the largest one is the elephant seal. (**T**) It weighs up to four tons! (**U**) A well-known antarctic bird is the penguin. (**V**) Instead of flying, these birds stand and waddle on flippers. (**W**) Most people think penguins look funny. (**X**) Maybe this is because these people think that penguins look like humans dressed up in tuxedos. (**Y**) Maybe people look as funny to penguins as they look to us!

1. What did the ice do to plant and animal life on Antarctica?
   Sentence   **(A)**   **(B)**   **(C)**   **(D)**

2. Are there many living things in Antarctica?
   Sentence   **(A)**   **(B)**   **(C)**   **(D)**

3. Are land animals ever seen?
   Sentence   **(E)**   **(F)**   **(G)**   **(H)**

4. What kind of fossils have explorers found?
   Sentence   **(H)**   **(I)**   **(J)**   **(K)**

5. What is the length of the largest land animal?
   Sentence   **(J)**   **(K)**   **(L)**   **(M)**

6. Where do most animals in Antarctica live?
   Sentence   **(L)**   **(M)**   **(N)**   **(O)**

7. What is the largest creature that has ever lived?
   Sentence   **(M)**   **(N)**   **(O)**   **(P)**

8. Do blue whales have teeth?
   Sentence   **(Q)**   **(R)**   **(S)**   **(T)**

9. What is a well-known Antarctic bird?
   Sentence   **(T)**   **(U)**   **(V)**   **(W)**

10. Why might people think that penguins look funny?
    Sentence   **(U)**   **(V)**   **(W)**   **(X)**

(A) The country that touches the United States the most is Canada. (B) This giant land borders on over a dozen U.S. states. (C) You can walk across the border from eleven states. (D) You can sail right across the border from three others. (E) Canada is the second largest country in the world. (F) Only the former Soviet Union ("Russia") is bigger.

(G) Canada covers most of the northern part of North America. (H) It sits on top of the United States like a big hat on a head. (I) So big is Canada that it stretches one-quarter of the way around the world. (J) Most of its coastline is very rocky. (K) On the east it meets the Atlantic Ocean, on the west the Pacific Ocean, and on the north the Arctic Ocean. (L) The Arctic shores of Canada are so close to the North Pole that instead of waves there is usually only ice.

(M) Even though Canada is so large, it does not have a great many people. (N) Much of the country is covered with endless forests and partly frozen land called tundra. (O) Most of Canada's people live in the south, near the United States, where the weather is not so cold.

(P) It is a good thing that Canada and the United States have long been friends. (Q) The borderline between the two countries is over five thousand miles long. (R) Yet they never have to keep soldiers along this border. (S) The countries never worry about going to war with each other.

(T) With all its land and ocean shores, Canada can supply many things the world needs. (U) Wood from its trees makes paper for newspapers and books. (V) Valuable oil is pumped from underground in the west. (W) The central plains grow millions of bushels of wheat. (X) Along Canada's shores lie some of the richest fishing grounds in the world. (Y) In the Atlantic fishers catch codfish, lobster, herring, and mackerel. (Z) In the Pacific they catch salmon, halibut, and shellfish.

1. What country borders the United States more than any other?
   Sentence　(A)　　　(B)　　　(C)　　　(D)

2. How many U.S. states does Canada border?
   Sentence　(B)　　　(C)　　　(D)　　　(E)

3. Is it possible to sail across the Canadian border?
   Sentence　(D)　　　(E)　　　(F)　　　(G)

4. Why is Canada compared to a hat?
   Sentence　(E)　　　(F)　　　(G)　　　(H)

5. Are there three oceans bordering Canada?
   Sentence　(I)　　　(J)　　　(K)　　　(L)

6. What are the Arctic shores of Canada near?
   Sentence　(J)　　　(K)　　　(L)　　　(M)

7. What is the frozen land called?
   Sentence　(N)　　　(O)　　　(P)　　　(Q)

8. Is the threat of war ever a worry between the U.S. and Canada?
   Sentence　(R)　　　(S)　　　(T)　　　(U)

9. What valuable product can be found underground?
   Sentence　(T)　　　(U)　　　(V)　　　(W)

10. Does the Pacific Ocean provide many fish?
    Sentence　(W)　　　(X)　　　(Y)　　　(Z)

(A) If you visited many parts of Canada, you might think you were still in the United States. (B) Most of the people look the same, talk the same, and wear the same kinds of clothes as Americans do. (C) Only the Canadian flag would tell you that you were in a different country. (D) Canada's flag is white with a big red maple leaf in the center and red bars at each end.

(E) Most of Canada's people speak English. (F) But about one person of every three speaks French. (G) This is because over three hundred years ago some people from France crossed the Atlantic Ocean to settle in Canada. (H) Most of them settled in an area called Quebec. (I) Quebec is in eastern Canada. (J) It lies just across the border from New York State and New England.

(K) Most people in Quebec still speak French today. (L) Some towns in Quebec look just like French towns. (M) In Quebec, the biggest city is Montreal. (N) It is the largest French-speaking city in the world, outside of Paris.

(O) Western Canada is very much like western United States. (P) Cowhands ride the range and hold rodeos. (Q) A large population of Native Americans (Indians) still live in the Canadian West. (R) Many of them still follow old ways. (S) Even people from China and Japan make their homes along the west coast.

(T) Canada is also the homeland of Eskimos. (U) Many of them speak the Eskimo language. (V) Many of these Eskimos still live in the frozen Arctic. (W) They hunt seals, walruses, fish, and caribou. (X) From these creatures the Eskimos get food, as well as skins for clothing. (Y) Eskimos are among the best hunters in the world. (Z) Canada is truly a land of many different kinds of people.

1. What color are the bars at each end of Canada's flag?
   Sentence   (**A**)   (**B**)   (**C**)   (**D**)

2. What language do most Canadians speak?
   Sentence   (**C**)   (**D**)   (**E**)   (**F**)

3. What ocean did some people from France cross to reach Canada?
   Sentence   (**F**)   (**G**)   (**H**)   (**I**)

4. Was Quebec the area in which these people settled?
   Sentence   (**H**)   (**I**)   (**J**)   (**K**)

5. Do most people in Quebec speak English?
   Sentence   (**I**)   (**J**)   (**K**)   (**L**)

6. What is the largest city in Quebec?
   Sentence   (**L**)   (**M**)   (**N**)   (**O**)

7. Do Native Americans live in any part of Canada?
   Sentence   (**O**)   (**P**)   (**Q**)   (**R**)

8. Do Eskimos have a language of their own?
   Sentence   (**R**)   (**S**)   (**T**)   (**U**)

9. Are Eskimos known to catch fish?
   Sentence   (**U**)   (**V**)   (**W**)   (**X**)

10. Are the people of Canada all alike?
    Sentence   (**W**)   (**X**)   (**Y**)   (**Z**)

(**A**) Nature has been good to Canada. (**B**) It is not only a big country, but it is also a beautiful one. (**C**) Its forests, mountains, lakes, plains, and shores delight both Canadians and visitors.

(**D**) On the Atlantic coast lie many lovely beaches and seaside hills. (**E**) Visitors to the Bay of Fundy can see the highest tides in the world. (**F**) The waters sometimes rise over fifty feet at high tide. (**G**) That is deep enough to cover a five-story building.

(**H**) Ontario is the part of Canada lying just above the Great Lakes. (**I**) It contains thousands of lakes for fishing, swimming, and boating. (**J**) Canada has more lakes than any other country in the world. (**K**) On Ontario's border with the United States is Niagara Falls. (**L**) The waters of the Niagara River fall 158 feet in a cloud of mist and spray.

(**M**) The middle of Canada is largely covered with fields of wheat and other grains. (**N**) In winter boys and girls play hockey on outdoor ice rinks. (**O**) Sometimes the temperature drops to fifty degrees below zero Fahrenheit.

(**P**) Western Canada has the great snow-capped peaks of the Rocky Mountains. (**Q**) Banff Park is famous for its beautiful mountain lakes, green valleys, ice fields, and hot springs. (**R**) People come from all over the world to see the natural wonders of Banff, Lake Louise, Glacier Park, and Jasper Park.

(**S**) Canada's Pacific coast is over 5,500 miles long. (**T**) Warm ocean waters make parts of the west very pleasant for living. (**U**) Winters there are warmer than elsewhere in Canada. (**V**) People there need good raincoats and umbrellas, though. (**W**) Some places on the Pacific coast receive over a hundred inches of rain a year.

(**X**) Because it touches three oceans, Canada has the world's longest coastline. (**Y**) It adds up to nearly sixty thousand miles. (**Z**) Walking all of Canada's shores would be longer than walking around the world twice!

UNIT 16
Canada—Blessed by Nature

1. Is Canada considered a beautiful country?
   Sentence   (**A**)   (**B**)   (**C**)   (**D**)

2. Can visitors see something unusual at the Bay of Fundy?
   Sentence   (**D**)   (**E**)   (**F**)   (**G**)

3. Where is Niagara Falls located?
   Sentence   (**H**)   (**I**)   (**J**)   (**K**)

4. Is there a great drop to the Niagara Falls?
   Sentence   (**J**)   (**K**)   (**L**)   (**M**)

5. Are the temperatures very cold in the middle of Canada?
   Sentence   (**M**)   (**N**)   (**O**)   (**P**)

6. Where might you find ice fields and hot springs in one area?
   Sentence   (**O**)   (**P**)   (**Q**)   (**R**)

7. Is Lake Louise near Jasper Park?
   Sentence   (**Q**)   (**R**)   (**S**)   (**T**)

8. Is Canada bordered on the west by the Pacific Ocean?
   Sentence   (**S**)   (**T**)   (**U**)   (**V**)

9. Does much rain fall in western Canada?
   Sentence   (**U**)   (**V**)   (**W**)   (**X**)

10. What is the length of Canada's coastline?
    Sentence   (**W**)   (**X**)   (**Y**)   (**Z**)

(**A**) Half a world away from us lies the land known as Australia. (**B**) This is the place where a baby animal lives in its mother's pocket and a bird laughs instead of singing. (**C**) Since Australia is near the bottom of the globe, it is often called "the land down under."

(**D**) Australia is really too large to be called just an island. (**E**) It is really an island continent. (**F**) Australia is the only continent that is all one country. (**G**) The northern coast of Australia lies nearest the equator. (**H**) It is the warmest part of the country. (**I**) The southern section is closest to the South Pole and is the coolest.

(**J**) Much of Australia is not suited to comfortable living. (**K**) About one third of it, the central and western parts, contains a large desert where little rain falls. (**L**) Few people live in the north. (**M**) It is far too warm. (**N**) Most people prefer the cooler eastern and south-eastern sections.

(**O**) Australia is a leader in raising sheep. (**P**) Sheep, in fact, out-number people nine to one. (**Q**) Australia supplies about one-third of the world's wool. (**R**) Wool is easily the nation's largest money-maker. (**S**) Sheep ranches, called "stations," dot the country. (**T**) So great is the distance between these stations that people often live many miles from their nearest neighbor.

(**U**) Australia, in spite of its large size, has a small population. (**V**) Its chief need is people. (**W**) Much of the land is empty because there aren't enough people to develop its riches. (**X**) For many years Australians have been asking others to move to their land. (**Y**) Many people have accepted that offer in recent years. (**Z**) There is still plenty of room if you would like a new home.

1. Is there a laughing bird in Australia?
   Sentence   (A)   (B)   (C)   (D)

2. Which coast of Australia is closest to the equator?
   Sentence   (E)   (F)   (G)   (H)

3. Which part of Australia is nearest the South Pole?
   Sentence   (H)   (I)   (J)   (K)

4. Why do few people live in the north?
   Sentence   (L)   (M)   (N)   (O)

5. In which parts of Australia do most people like to live?
   Sentence   (N)   (O)   (P)   (Q)

6. Does Australia have more people or more sheep?
   Sentence   (P)   (Q)   (R)   (S)

7. What are sheep ranches called?
   Sentence   (R)   (S)   (T)   (U)

8. Are the stations close together?
   Sentence   (T)   (U)   (V)   (W)

9. What does Australia need more than anything else?
   Sentence   (V)   (W)   (X)   (Y)

10. Are more people settling in Australia today?
    Sentence   (W)   (X)   (Y)   (Z)

UNIT 18
Life in Australia

(**A**) Australia, an island continent, is on the other side of the world from North America. (**B**) It might surprise you to know that Australians live like Americans in many ways.

(**C**) We might have trouble understanding the Australian accent, but we know the language. (**D**) Most Australians speak English. (**E**) Like people in America or Canada, they live in cities, towns, and farms. (**F**) And like us, many Australians love outdoor sports. (**G**) Water sports such as swimming, boating, and surfing are favorites.

(**H**) Most Australians or their ancestors came to Australia from Europe. (**I**) The native Australians, or aborigines (say "ab or RIJ in eez"), have lived in Australia for about forty thousand years. (**J**) But the Europeans took over much of the land when they came to Australia. (**K**) This made life difficult for the aborigines. (**L**) Today, however, many people are working for the rights of the aborigines.

(**M**) Most Australians live in cities near the coast. (**N**) A huge area of land in the middle of Australia has very few people living on it. (**O**) Australians call this wide, open land the "Great Outback." (**P**) Huge sheep ranches are located in the Outback. (**Q**) Sometimes the distance between ranches is so great that people do not see their neighbors for months at a time.

(**R**) What else is unusual about the Outback? (**S**) Children there "go to school" by staying at home! (**T**) Often the nearest school is hundreds of miles away. (**U**) The children listen and talk to a teacher on a two-way radio that sends and receives messages. (**V**) This school is known as the School of the Air. (**W**) Children do their schoolwork at home. (**X**) Then they mail their papers to their teachers. (**Y**) Children must be well-behaved in this "school at home"—their parents are watching!

1. Is life in Australia anything like life in America?
    Sentence   **(A)**   **(B)**   **(C)**   **(D)**

2. Do Australians speak English with an accent?
    Sentence   **(C)**   **(D)**   **(E)**   **(F)**

3. Do Australians like indoor or outdoor sports?
    Sentence   **(E)**   **(F)**   **(G)**   **(H)**

4. What are the people who are native Australians called?
    Sentence   **(G)**   **(H)**   **(I)**   **(J)**

5. Do many people live in the middle of Australia?
    Sentence   **(K)**   **(L)**   **(M)**   **(N)**

6. Where are there many sheep ranches?
    Sentence   **(N)**   **(O)**   **(P)**   **(Q)**

7. Why don't people on ranches see their neighbors very often?
    Sentence   **(P)**   **(Q)**   **(R)**   **(S)**

8. How do the children in the Outback talk to their teachers?
    Sentence   **(S)**   **(T)**   **(U)**   **(V)**

9. What is the school called?
    Sentence   **(U)**   **(V)**   **(W)**   **(X)**

10. What encourages children to be well-behaved in this school?
    Sentence   **(V)**   **(W)**   **(X)**   **(Y)**

(**A**) Australia is known for its strange animals. (**B**) Some of these animals are different from those found anywhere in the world. (**C**) Many of them are called marsupials—animals that are carried in a pouch by their mothers.

(**D**) The largest of the marsupials is the kangaroo. (**E**) A big "boomer" kangaroo may stand over six feet tall and weigh three hundred pounds. (**F**) It can leap twenty-five feet in a single jump. (**G**) It bounds along at thirty-five miles per hour. (**H**) Oddly enough, a newborn kangaroo is not much longer than a person's fingernail!

(**I**) Perhaps the strangest animal is the platypus. (**J**) This animal has webbed feet, a soft bill shaped like a duck's, and a tail like a beaver's. (**K**) It is very shy and lives mostly in or near the water. (**L**) The platypus is so strange-looking that it has to be seen to be believed.

(**M**) Australia is also the home of an unusual bird called the kookaburra. (**N**) The kookaburra isn't afraid of people. (**O**) It will fly within inches of young and old without the slightest worry. (**P**) This bird is known for an unusual habit. (**Q**) Instead of singing, the kookaburra lets out a crazy laugh! (**R**) This bird is sometimes called the laughing jackass.

(**S**) It isn't known why so many odd animals live in Australia. (**T**) Perhaps it's because Australia is so far away from any other large land. (**U**) The animals have thus been left to their own special ways for a long time. (**V**) As time has passed, the animals have changed. (**W**) The changes have been slow. (**X**) Animals have become better fitted for life there. (**Y**) They have also grown quite different from animals of other lands. (**Z**) People interested in animals would surely find Australia worth visiting.

1. What is a marsupial?
    Sentence   (A)   (B)   (C)   (D)

2. Is the kangaroo a marsupial?
    Sentence   (C)   (D)   (E)   (F)

3. How large is a newborn kangaroo?
    Sentence   (E)   (F)   (G)   (H)

4. Does the platypus have a tail like a beaver's?
    Sentence   (H)   (I)   (J)   (K)

5. Where does a platypus live?
    Sentence   (J)   (K)   (L)   (M)

6. What is a kookaburra?
    Sentence   (L)   (M)   (N)   (O)

7. How close to people does the kookaburra fly?
    Sentence   (N)   (O)   (P)   (Q)

8. What is another name for kookaburra?
    Sentence   (Q)   (R)   (S)   (T)

9. Is it known why so many strange animals live in Australia?
    Sentence   (S)   (T)   (U)   (V)

10. Would animal lovers find Australia worth visiting?
    Sentence   (W)   (X)   (Y)   (Z)

A. Exercising Your Skill

In Units 14 through 19 you read passages about the country of Canada and the continent of Australia. In these passages, you read facts about landforms, temperatures, and rainfall in different parts of these lands. These kinds of information are often shown on charts or graphs.

Look at the bar graph below. It shows the average amounts of rainfall in inches for certain months. Study the graph. Then read the questions that follow the graph. On your paper write only the questions that can be answered with information in the graph.

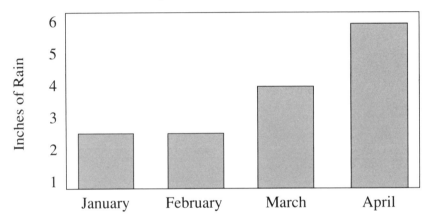

Average Rainfall in Springtown

1. How many inches of rain fell in February?
2. Which month had 4 inches of rain?
3. Which of the four months listed had the most rain?
4. How much rain did Springtown have in April?
5. Which two months had the same amount of rain?

B. Expanding Your Skill

You have probably seen bar graphs in your social studies books. Work with two or three classmates. Together make up a list of the kinds of things you have seen listed on bar graphs. Look in your schoolbooks if you need help. Write the final group list on your paper. Compare your group's list with other lists in the class.

C. Exploring Language

Look at the following bar graph. Work with a partner. Each of you should write five questions that can be answered with information from the graph. Write the questions and exchange papers. See how quickly you can answer each other's questions.

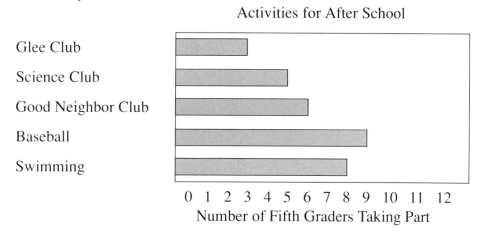

Activities for After School

Glee Club

Science Club

Good Neighbor Club

Baseball

Swimming

0 1 2 3 4 5 6 7 8 9 10 11 12
Number of Fifth Graders Taking Part

D. Expressing Yourself

Choose one of these activities.

1. Make up a bar graph that you can fill in during the week. Make your graph show the average number of hours you spend playing outside. The left column down can show "Hours per Day." The line across the bottom can show "Days of the Week." Compare your graph with your classmates' graphs.

2. Graphs are like "word pictures." Create a word graph for the seasons. In the left column number up from one to ten. In a line across the bottom write *January, April, July,* and *October.* Above each month write words that describe the month. When you are done, the words will form a bar graph that tells what you think about the four seasons.

UNIT 20
Egypt, Gift of the Nile

(**A**) Egypt is a large Arab land located mostly in the northeastern part of Africa. (**B**) A small part of Egypt is in Asia, at the place where Asia and Africa meet. (**C**) So Egypt is really in two continents. (**D**) The part in Asia is called the Sinai Peninsula. (**E**) Once the Sinai was connected to the rest of Egypt. (**F**) Then in the 1860s a great canal was cut between the Sinai and the rest of Egypt. (**G**) It is called the Suez Canal.

(**H**) Egypt contains part of the world's largest and hottest desert, the Sahara. (**I**) Very little of Egypt is good for settlement. (**J**) Most of the land is covered by sand. (**K**) People must cluster around the few places where they can find water. (**L**) Few people want to live out in the desert. (**M**) Most choose to live along the banks of the Nile River.

(**N**) The valley of the Nile, which is less than ten miles wide, is surrounded on both sides by blazing deserts. (**O**) Little farming is carried on outside of the Nile area. (**P**) For thousands of years it has been the Nile that has brought water to the Egyptians. (**Q**) Without the Nile Egypt could not live.

(**R**) Away from the Nile there is little water. (**S**) Summer and winter the sun shines in a cloudless sky. (**T**) Some Egyptians live their entire lives without ever seeing rain. (**U**) As much as ten to thirty years may pass without a single shower.

(**V**) Even though the growing area along the Nile is small, many fine crops are raised. (**W**) The most important crop is cotton. (**X**) Egyptian cotton is among the finest grown in the world. (**Y**) Wheat, barley, and corn are other crops raised along the river. (**Z**) These crops, like Egypt itself, are the "Gift of the Nile."

1. What country is really in two continents?
   Sentence   (A)   (B)   (C)   (D)

2. Where is the Sinai Peninsula?
   Sentence   (B)   (C)   (D)   (E)

3. When was a canal cut?
   Sentence   (D)   (E)   (F)   (G)

4. What is the name for the world's largest desert?
   Sentence   (F)   (G)   (H)   (I)

5. Is much of Egypt covered by sand?
   Sentence   (I)   (J)   (K)   (L)

6. Where do most Egyptians live?
   Sentence   (L)   (M)   (N)   (O)

7. How many miles wide is the Nile River Valley?
   Sentence   (N)   (O)   (P)   (Q)

8. Does the sun shine in the winter?
   Sentence   (Q)   (R)   (S)   (T)

9. What is Egypt's most important crop?
   Sentence   (T)   (U)   (V)   (W)

10. Is corn grown along the Nile?
    Sentence   (W)   (X)   (Y)   (Z)

(**A**) One-third of Egyptians are farmers. (**B**) They live a hard life. (**C**) They work in the fields from sunrise to sunset. (**D**) Quite often the whole family—parents and children—work in the field together. (**E**) As darkness falls, the family returns to its mud-brick hut. (**F**) Farm animals live in the hut along with the family.

(**G**) Whatever worries a farm family may have, the problem of who's going to do the dishes is not one of them. (**H**) There are no dishes to clean. (**I**) Egyptian farm families do not use dishes at meal-time. (**J**) They use a piece of bread as a scoop. (**K**) After each person has scooped from the pot, the piece of bread is eaten. (**L**) There is no waste of food.

(**M**) The summer heat is a problem. (**N**) During warm summer nights, city people like to spend as much time out-of-doors as possible. (**O**) They walk about the streets until late hours. (**P**) Sometimes when it is simply too warm to sleep indoors, people take their beds outside their homes! (**Q**) It is different during the hot afternoons. (**R**) At this time, when the sun's rays are the hottest, people go home and take an afternoon nap.

(**S**) Egyptians enjoy many of the same foods that we eat. (**T**) They like tomatoes, dates, lemons, and oranges. (**U**) Their chief food is porridge. (**V**) It is made with brown beans. (**W**) Tasty, roasted ears of corn, which are very popular, can be bought from vendors on the streets.

(**X**) People in Egypt like music. (**Y**) Their music is very different from that heard in America. (**Z**) Their children's games of tag, jump rope, and hide-and-seek, however, show that children are much alike the world over.

1. Do Egyptian farmers live a hard life?
   Sentence   **(A)**   **(B)**   **(C)**   **(D)**

2. Do Egyptian children help with the work?
   Sentence   **(C)**   **(D)**   **(E)**   **(F)**

3. Where do the farm animals live?
   Sentence   **(E)**   **(F)**   **(G)**   **(H)**

4. What is used as a scoop for food?
   Sentence   **(G)**   **(H)**   **(I)**   **(J)**

5. Do Egyptians eat the bread?
   Sentence   **(I)**   **(J)**   **(K)**   **(L)**

6. Do Egyptians sleep outdoors?
   Sentence   **(M)**   **(N)**   **(O)**   **(P)**

7. Where do the people go in the afternoons?
   Sentence   **(O)**   **(P)**   **(Q)**   **(R)**

8. Are oranges eaten in Egypt?
   Sentence   **(R)**   **(S)**   **(T)**   **(U)**

9. What is the chief Egyptian food?
   Sentence   **(U)**   **(V)**   **(W)**   **(X)**

10. Is Egyptian music like ours?
    Sentence   **(W)**   **(X)**   **(Y)**   **(Z)**

(A) The pyramids of Egypt are exciting. (B) They trace back far into the past. (C) How old they are nobody knows. (D) The Great Pyramid at Giza is said to have been built more than 4,500 years ago!

(E) People wonder why pyramids were built. (F) The answer has to do with the religion of the Egyptians. (G) They believed in a life after death. (H) The pyramids were built as tombs for the dead Egyptian pharaohs, or rulers. (I) All that the pharaohs would need in their second lives was placed inside the pyramids.

(J) Pyramids were built not just anywhere. (K) They had to be built near the Nile River. (L) The river was used as a water highway. (M) The huge blocks of limestone used to build the pyramids were floated across the river on rafts.

(N) What a job it must have been without the tools of today! (O) The work was done largely by human muscle power. (P) Each stone was higher than a person. (Q) Each weighed as much as a truck. (R) Over two million of these stones were used to build a single pyramid. (S) It is believed that it took fifty slaves to pull a single stone along. (T) Perhaps as many as 100,000 slaves worked for twenty years to build the Great Pyramid.

(U) The pyramids have changed some from the time they were first built. (V) They are not quite as tall now. (W) Over the years some of the stones have been taken away. (X) People wanted them for their own use. (Y) The sides of the pyramids are no longer smooth as they once were. (Z) Even so, the "Mountains of the Pharaohs," as the pyramids are called by the Arabs, make all who look at them marvel at the skill of the Egyptians who lived so long ago.

1. How long ago was the Great Pyramid at Giza built?
   Sentence   (A)   (B)   (C)   (D)

2. Did the Egyptians believe in a life after death?
   Sentence   (E)   (F)   (G)   (H)

3. Why were the pyramids built?
   Sentence   (G)   (H)   (I)   (J)

4. Near what body of water were the pyramids built?
   Sentence   (I)   (J)   (K)   (L)

5. What kind of stone was used to build the pyramids?
   Sentence   (L)   (M)   (N)   (O)

6. How much did each stone weigh?
   Sentence   (N)   (O)   (P)   (Q)

7. How many slaves were needed to pull a stone along?
   Sentence   (Q)   (R)   (S)   (T)

8. How long did it take to build the Great Pyramid?
   Sentence   (S)   (T)   (U)   (V)

9. Are the pyramids as tall as they once were?
   Sentence   (U)   (V)   (W)   (X)

10. What do the Arabs call the pyramids?
    Sentence   (W)   (X)   (Y)   (Z)

UNIT 23
Amazing Brazil

(A) "Amazing" is the word for Brazil. (B) No other word can describe the country quite so well. (C) Those who visit the South American land soon learn why. (D) In all the world only four countries are larger. (E) Shaped like a triangle, Brazil is as wide as it is long. (F) It borders every country in South America except two.

(G) Brazil is big in more than just size. (H) It is a giant when it comes to growing crops. (I) Its rich soil has made it the world's leading country in growing coffee and in producing sugar.

(J) An airplane flight across Brazil shows how different one part of the country is from another. (K) Wide plains, hills, mountains, and dense forests stretch across the land. (L) Most of Brazil, however, is covered by a thick forest. (M) Seen from the air, it looks like a dark green blanket. (N) No larger forest is found anywhere in the world, not even in Africa.

(O) The people of Brazil are of many different religions. (P) They are also of several different races. (Q) There are whites, blacks, and Indians. (R) There are people from Portugal, Italy, Spain, Germany, and many other countries. (S) Over half of Brazil's people are of Portuguese ancestry. (T) The main language spoken is Portuguese.

(U) One of the world's most beautiful cities, Rio de Janeiro, is found in Brazil. (V) Old houses stand alongside modern buildings. (W) Rio is dotted with parks, fountains, and bright sidewalks. (X) Many of the pavements are made from bright little pieces of tile. (Y) These pieces of baked clay fit together to form pretty patterns. (Z) A walk in Rio is a walk of delight.

1. What word describes Brazil?
   Sentence   (A)   (B)   (C)   (D)

2. How many countries are larger than Brazil?
   Sentence   (C)   (D)   (E)   (F)

3. What shape does Brazil have?
   Sentence   (E)   (F)   (G)   (H)

4. Why is Brazil a leader in growing crops?
   Sentence   (G)   (H)   (I)   (J)

5. Are there any mountains in Brazil?
   Sentence   (I)   (J)   (K)   (L)

6. What covers most of Brazil?
   Sentence   (L)   (M)   (N)   (O)

7. Is Africa's forestland larger than Brazil's?
   Sentence   (N)   (O)   (P)   (Q)

8. Of what ancestry are most of Brazil's people?
   Sentence   (P)   (Q)   (R)   (S)

9. Does Rio have any parks?
   Sentence   (T)   (U)   (V)   (W)

10. From what are many of the pavements made?
    Sentence   (W)   (X)   (Y)   (Z)

UNIT 24
Living in Brazil

(A) People are always surprised when they learn that rice is the chief food of Brazilians. (B) It is eaten by nearly everyone, those in the cities and those on the farms. (C) Vegetables are often cooked with the rice to add flavor. (D) Turtle meat is another food that Brazilians find tasty. (E) Brazilians are as fond of steak as people in our own country are.

(F) It should not be difficult to guess the favorite drink of the people living in the world's leading coffee producer. (G) It's coffee, of course. (H) However, many people are fond of tea also. (I) Cowhands in Brazil like tea so much that they even carry it with them. (J) They drink tea through straws, much as we drink sodas. (K) Each cowhand carries tea, a metal straw, and a pot while riding the range. (L) The pot is used to boil the tea water.

(M) Few people enjoy holidays more than Brazilians. (N) The most important holiday is Carnival. (O) Everything stops for this three-day holiday. (P) Places of business close, and all work comes to a halt. (Q) Carnival is the time for music, parties, parades, and dances. (R) Everyone dances—from toddlers to grandparents—and right in the street.

(S) In the past, fewer than half of the people in Brazil could read or write. (T) Many of the older people had no chance to attend school. (U) Today, however, elementary education is free. (V) The law says that all children must go to school for at least the first eight grades.

(W) Many of the people of Brazil are very poor. (X) Sometimes it takes a year for a person to make as much money as the average American makes in one month. (Y) Better jobs, houses, and living conditions are needed. (Z) Brazil is working hard to solve this problem of poverty.

1. What is the chief food eaten by the people of Brazil?
   Sentence   (A)   (B)   (C)   (D)

2. Why are vegetables added to the rice?
   Sentence   (C)   (D)   (E)   (F)

3. Do people in Brazil like steak?
   Sentence   (E)   (F)   (G)   (H)

4. What is the favorite drink of Brazilians?
   Sentence   (G)   (H)   (I)   (J)

5. How do Brazilians drink tea?
   Sentence   (I)   (J)   (K)   (L)

6. What is the most important holiday?
   Sentence   (K)   (L)   (M)   (N)

7. How long does Carnival last?
   Sentence   (M)   (N)   (O)   (P)

8. Who dances in the streets?
   Sentence   (P)   (Q)   (R)   (S)

9. Why are many older people unable to read or write?
   Sentence   (S)   (T)   (U)   (V)

10. Is Brazil trying to solve the problem of poverty?
   Sentence   (W)   (X)   (Y)   (Z)

(**A**) "It's more like an ocean than a river." (**B**) That is what the people of Brazil say about their Amazon River. (**C**) There is truth in what they say. (**D**) Nowhere on earth is there a river so mighty. (**E**) The river's flow is twelve times as great as our Mississippi's. (**F**) The Amazon is fittingly called the "Greatest of Waters."

(**G**) The Amazon begins its journey high in the Andes Mountains, two hundred miles from the Pacific Ocean. (**H**) It slowly winds and twists for a thousand miles before its muddy-brown waters spill from its mouth into the Atlantic Ocean. (**I**) What a mouth it has! (**J**) The mouth is over two hundred miles wide. (**K**) An island in the mouth is as big as Holland.

(**L**) Not many people live along the banks of the river. (**M**) The climate is much too hot for most people. (**N**) Besides, the river's banks are covered by vines and trees. (**O**) This forest provides a home for wild animals.

(**P**) Here there are insects of every kind and shape, some as large as birds. (**Q**) Blood-sucking vampire bats hide in the trees. (**R**) Monkeys chatter in the trees, alligators sun themselves on the riverbanks, and snakes grow so large they can swallow a deer whole.

(**S**) How mighty is the mighty Amazon? (**T**) You might get an idea from the following fact. (**U**) In less time than it took you to read this story, the Amazon pumped three billion gallons of water into the Atlantic Ocean. (**V**) How much water is that? (**W**) It is more than one gallon for every person on earth. (**X**) All this takes place in less than a minute. (**Y**) This goes on each minute of each hour, day and night, year after year. (**Z**) The Greatest of Waters never rests.

1. What do people say about the Amazon River?
    Sentence   (A)   (B)   (C)   (D)

2. How does the river's flow compare with the Mississippi's?
    Sentence   (C)   (D)   (E)   (F)

3. What is another name given to the Amazon?
    Sentence   (E)   (F)   (G)   (H)

4. Where does the Amazon begin its journey?
    Sentence   (G)   (H)   (I)   (J)

5. Is there any island in the Amazon's mouth?
    Sentence   (I)   (J)   (K)   (L)

6. Why don't most people like the climate along the river?
    Sentence   (K)   (L)   (M)   (N)

7. How large are some of the insects along the riverbank?
    Sentence   (M)   (N)   (O)   (P)

8. What can the snakes eat?
    Sentence   (Q)   (R)   (S)   (T)

9. Where does the water of the Amazon go?
    Sentence   (T)   (U)   (V)   (W)

10. Does the Amazon ever rest?
    Sentence   (W)   (X)   (Y)   (Z)

A. Exercising Your Skill

In Units 20 through Unit 25 you read passages about Egypt and Brazil. Some television stations run special programs on countries such as these.

Study this advertisement for a television special. Then read the list of questions. On your paper write only the questions that could probably be answered by watching the program.

Thursday, March 30   8:00 - 9:00 P.M.

Don't miss the spectacular   **LIFE IN ANCIENT EGYPT**
              Learn about . . .   • the life of the pharaohs
                                          • the life of the scribes (teachers)
                                          • the life of the common people

---

1. What kinds of ceremonies did the pharaohs have?
2. What is life like for an ordinary family in Egypt today?
3. How do modern Egyptians make a living?
4. How did the common people dress in ancient Egypt?
5. How were ancient Egyptian boats made?
6. Where did the Egyptian pharaohs live in ancient times?
7. How did the scribes work?
8. Who discovered what Egyptian picture writing meant?
9. Could common people in ancient Egypt read and write?
10. Where did the scribes live?

B. Expanding Your Skill

What are some things you can learn from a television special about a country? Work with a group of classmates. Look at a television program guide for ideas and make a group list of such things. Compare your group's list with other lists in the class.

C. Exploring Language

Look at this section of program listings for a television station. Think of ten questions that could be answered from information in the listings. The questions can be about the dates, the times, or the programs. Write the questions on your paper. Compare your questions with your classmates' questions.

SPECIALS FOR APRIL

Tuesday **Brazil—The Emerald Triangle**
April 4 Forest, cities, people, and celebrations
7 - 8 P.M.

Thursday **Canada—Land of Many Provinces**
April 13 Quebec, Ontario, and British Columbia
8 - 9 P.M.

Tuesday **Australia—The Animals of The Land Down Under**
April 18 The koala, the kangaroo—and more
8 - 9 P.M.

Sunday **India—Many Lives**
April 23 A look at the lives of villagers, teachers, and farmers
4 - 5 P.M.

D. Expressing Yourself

Choose one of these activities.

1. Clip a section of a television program listing from a newspaper and paste it on a sheet of paper. Write five questions about the dates, times, and titles of the shows given in the listing. Exchange papers with a classmate. See how long it takes each of you to find the answers to the questions.

2. Make up an advertisement for two television programs that you would like to see in the next month. Give the dates, the times, the program titles, and a brief description of each program. Draw a picture to go with each program.